The
Gospel of John
from

The Global
BIBLE™
FOR CHILDREN

Global Contemporary English Version

Authentic

How to use
The Gospel of John *and* The Global Bible for Children

This Bible was created just for you! Here are some of the special features you'll find in this Bible:

The Global Contemporary English Version
The pictures are pretty, but the Bible text is the most important part of this Bible. It is God's Word, written for you in a translation that is easy to understand.

Book Introductions
Short introductions to the books of the Bible are easy to read and give you an overview of the writer, intended audience, and theme of each book.

Full-Color Photographs
Bright, colorful photographs introduce you to other children your age, different animals, and interesting locations from around the world.

Fact File and Fun Facts
Pages that introduce a country or continent will have a Fact File including population, languages, and a description of what features make it unique. Fun Facts let you know fascinating characteristics about each.

Did You Know? boxes
Look for these yellow boxes throughout the Bible. They contain little known trivia that you can learn and share with your friends.

Look It Up! boxes
These blue boxes feature quizzes and test your knowledge. Answers to these quizzes can be found by reading the country pages, continent pages, and the Bible text.

Maps
The Physical Map shows you how the world would look if you took a picture of it. The Political Map is an outline of each country showing you the borders and capitals.

Bible Dictionary
The Mini Dictionary for the Bible will help you understand the meaning of words you may not be familiar with.

Notes
The Notes at the end of every book of the Bible provide further information on text and translation issues.

John

The Gospel according to John stands apart from the other three Gospels. It opens with a Prologue in which Jesus is described as the Word of Life. The remainder of the book is organized around seven signs (miracles) that point to Jesus as the Son of God. This Gospel also reproduces a number of long conversations Jesus had with people in which he revealed who he was and what God had sent him to do.

The Word of Life

1 ¹ In the beginning was the one
who is called the Word.
The Word was with God
and was truly God.
² From the very beginning
the Word was with God.

³ And with this Word,
God created all things.
Nothing was made
without the Word.
Everything that was created
⁴ received its life from him,
and his life gave light
to everyone.
⁵ The light keeps shining
in the dark,
and darkness has never
put it out.°

⁶ God sent a man named John,
⁷ who came to tell
about the light
and to lead all people
to have faith.
⁸ John wasn't that light.
He came only to tell
about the light.

⁹ The true light that shines
on everyone
was coming into the world.
¹⁰ The Word was in the world,
but no one knew him,
though God had made the world
with his Word.
¹¹ He came into his own world,
but his own nation
did not welcome him.
¹² Yet some people accepted him
and put their faith in him.
So he gave them the right
to be the children of God.
¹³ They were not God's children

by nature or because
of any human desires.
God himself was the one
who made them his children.

¹⁴ The Word became
a human being
and lived here with us.
We saw his true glory,
the glory of the only Son
of the Father.
From him the complete gifts
of undeserved grace and truth
have come down to us.

¹⁵ John spoke about him and shouted, "This is the one I told you would come! He is greater than I am, because he was alive before I was born."

¹⁶ Because of all that the Son is, we have been given one blessing after another.° ¹⁷ The Law was given by Moses, but Jesus Christ brought us undeserved kindness and truth. ¹⁸ No one has ever seen God. The only Son, who is truly God and is closest to the Father, has shown us what God is like.

John the Baptist Tells about Jesus

¹⁹⁻²⁰ The religious authorities in Jerusalem sent priests and temple helpers to ask John who he was. He told them plainly, "I am not the Messiah." ²¹ Then when they asked him if he were Elijah, he said, "No, I am not!" And when they asked if he were the Prophet, he also said "No!"

²² Finally, they said, "Who are you then? We have to give an answer to the ones who sent us. Tell us who you are!"

²³ John answered in the words of the prophet Isaiah, "I am only someone shouting in the desert, 'Get the road ready for the Lord!' "

²⁴ Some Pharisees had also been sent to John. ²⁵ They asked him, "Why are you baptizing people, if you are not the Messiah or Elijah or the Prophet?"

²⁶ John told them, "I use water to baptize people. But here with you is someone you don't know. ²⁷ Even though I came first, I am not good enough

to untie his sandals." ²⁸ John said this as he was baptizing east of the Jordan River in Bethany.

The Lamb of God

²⁹ The next day, John saw Jesus coming toward him and said:

Here is the Lamb of God who takes away the sin of the world! ³⁰ He is the one I told you about when I said, "Someone else will come. He is greater than I am, because he was alive before I was born." ³¹ I didn't know who he was. But I came to baptize you with water, so that everyone in Israel would see him.

³² I was there and saw the Spirit come down on him like a dove from heaven. And the Spirit stayed on him. ³³ Before this I didn't know who he was. But the one who sent me to baptize with water had told me, "You will see the Spirit come down and stay on someone. Then you will know that he is the one who will baptize with the Holy Spirit." ³⁴ I saw this happen, and I tell you that he is the Son of God.

The First Disciples of Jesus

³⁵ The next day, John was there again, and two of his followers were with him. ³⁶ When he saw Jesus walking by, he said, "Here is the Lamb of God!" ³⁷ John's two followers heard him, and they went with Jesus.

³⁸ When Jesus turned and saw them, he asked, "What do you want?"

They answered, "Rabbi, where do you live?" The Hebrew word "Rabbi" means "Teacher."

³⁹ Jesus replied, "Come and see!" It was already about four o'clock in the afternoon when they went with him and saw where he lived. So they stayed on for the rest of the day.

⁴⁰ One of the two men who had heard John and had gone with Jesus was Andrew, the brother of Simon Peter. ⁴¹ The first thing Andrew did was to find his brother and tell him, "We have found the Messiah!" The Hebrew word "Messiah" means the same as the Greek word "Christ."

⁴² Andrew brought his brother to Jesus. And when Jesus saw him, he said, "Simon son of John, you will be called Cephas." This name can be translated as "Peter."

Jesus Chooses Philip and Nathanael

⁴³⁻⁴⁴ The next day Jesus decided to go to Galilee. There he met Philip, who was from Bethsaida, the hometown of Andrew and Peter. Jesus said to Philip, "Come with me."

⁴⁵ Philip then found Nathanael and said, "We have found the one that Moses and the Prophets wrote about. He is Jesus, the son of Joseph from Nazareth."

⁴⁶ Nathanael asked, "Can anything good come from Nazareth?"

Philip answered, "Come and see."

⁴⁷ When Jesus saw Nathanael coming toward him, he said, "Here is a true descendant of our ancestor Israel. And he isn't deceitful."

These girls in Mongolia love to play and dance in their classroom.

[48] "How do you know me?" Nathanael asked.

Jesus answered, "Before Philip called you, I saw you under the fig tree."

[49] Nathanael said, "Rabbi, you are the Son of God and the King of Israel!"

[50] Jesus answered, "Did you believe me just because I said that I saw you under the fig tree? You will see something even greater. [51] I tell you for certain that you will see heaven open and God's angels going up and coming down on the Son of Man."

Jesus at a Wedding in Cana

2 Three days later Mary, the mother of Jesus, was at a wedding feast in the village of Cana in Galilee. [2] Jesus and his disciples had also been invited and were there.

[3] When the wine was all gone, Mary said to Jesus, "They don't have any more wine."

[4] Jesus replied, "Mother, my time hasn't yet come! You must not tell me what to do."

[5] Mary then said to the servants, "Do whatever Jesus tells you to do."

[6] At the feast there were six stone water jars that were used by the people for washing themselves in the way that their religion said they must. Each jar held about 100 liters. [7] Jesus told the servants to fill them to the top with water. Then after the jars had been filled, [8] he said, "Now take some water and give it to the man in charge of the feast."

The servants did as Jesus told them, [9] and the man in charge drank some of the water that had now turned into wine. He did not know where the wine had come from, but the servants did. He called the bridegroom over [10] and said, "The best wine is always served first. Then after the guests have had plenty, the other wine is served. But you have kept the best until last!"

[11] This was Jesus' first miracle,° and he did it in the village of Cana in Galilee. There Jesus showed his glory, and his disciples put their faith in him. [12] After this, he went with his mother, his brothers, and his disciples to the town of Capernaum, where they stayed for a few days.

Jesus in the Temple

[13] Not long before the Jewish festival of Passover, Jesus went to Jerusalem. [14] There he found people selling cattle, sheep, and doves in the temple. He also saw moneychangers sitting at their tables. [15] So he took some rope and made a whip. Then he chased everyone out of the temple, together with their sheep and cattle. He turned over the tables of the moneychangers and scattered their coins.

[16] Jesus said to the people who had been selling doves, "Get those doves out of here! Don't make my Father's house a marketplace."

[17] The disciples then remembered that the Scriptures say, "My love for your house burns in me like a fire."

[18] The Jewish leaders asked Jesus, "What miracle° will you work to show us why you have done this?"

[19] "Destroy this temple," Jesus answered, "and in three days I will build it again!"

[20] The leaders replied, "It took 46 years to build this temple. What makes you think you can rebuild it in three days?"

[21] But Jesus was talking about his body as a temple. [22] And when he was raised from death, his disciples remembered what he had told them. Then they believed the Scriptures and the words of Jesus.

Jesus Knows What People Are Like

[23] In Jerusalem during Passover many people put their faith in Jesus, because they saw him work miracles.° [24] But Jesus knew what was in their hearts, and he would not let them have power over him. [25] No one had to tell him what people were like. He already knew.

Jesus and Nicodemus

3 There was a man named Nicodemus who was a Pharisee and a Jewish leader. [2] One night he went to Jesus and said, "Sir, we know that God has sent you to teach us. You could not work these miracles, unless God were with you."

[3] Jesus replied, "I tell you for certain that you must be born from above° before you can see God's kingdom!"

[4] Nicodemus asked, "How can a grown man ever be born a second time?"

[5] Jesus answered:

I tell you for certain that before you can get into God's kingdom, you must be born not only by water, but by the Spirit. [6] Humans give life to their children. Yet only God's Spirit can change you into a child of God. [7] Don't be surprised when I say that you must be born from above. [8] Only God's Spirit gives new life. The Spirit is like the wind that blows wherever it wants to. You can hear the wind, but you don't know where it comes from or where it is going.

[9] "How can this be?" Nicodemus asked.

[10] Jesus replied:

How can you be a teacher of Israel and not know these things? [11] I tell you for certain that we know what we are talking about because we have seen it ourselves. But none of you will accept what we say. [12] If you don't believe when I talk to you about things on earth, how can you possibly believe if I talk to you about things in heaven?

[13] No one has gone up to heaven except the Son of Man, who came down from there. [14] And the Son of Man must be lifted up, just as that metal snake was lifted up by Moses in the desert. [15] Then everyone who has faith in the Son of Man will have eternal life.

[16] God loved the people of this world so much that he gave his only Son, so that everyone who has faith in him will have eternal life and never really die. [17] God did not send his Son into the world to condemn its people. He sent him to save them! [18] No one who has faith in God's Son will be condemned. But everyone who doesn't have faith in him has already been condemned for not having faith in God's only Son.

[19] The light has come into the world, and people who do evil things are judged guilty because they love the dark more than the light. [20] People who do evil hate the light and won't come to the light, because it clearly shows what they have done. [21] But everyone who lives by the truth will come to the light, because they want others to know that God is really the one doing what they do.

Jesus and John the Baptist

[22] Later, Jesus and his disciples went to Judea, where he stayed with them for a while and was baptizing people.

[23-24] John had not yet been put in jail. He was at Aenon near Salim, where there was a lot of water, and people were coming there for John to baptize them.

[25] John's followers got into an argument with a Jewish man° about a ceremony of washing. [26] They went to John and said, "Rabbi, you spoke about a man when you were with him east of the Jordan. He is now baptizing people, and everyone is going to him."

[27] John replied:

No one can do anything unless God in heaven allows it. [28] You surely remember how I told you that I am not the Messiah. I am only the one sent ahead of him.

[29] At a wedding the groom is the one who gets married. The best man is glad just to be there and to hear the groom's voice. That's why I am so glad. [30] Jesus must become more important, while I become less important.

The One Who Comes from Heaven

[31] God's Son comes from heaven and is above all others. Everyone who comes from the earth belongs to the earth and speaks about earthly things. The one who comes from heaven is above all others. [32] He speaks about what he has seen and heard, and yet no one believes him. [33] But everyone who does believe him has shown that God is truthful. [34] The Son was sent to speak God's message, and he has been given the full power of God's Spirit.

[35] The Father loves the Son and has given him everything. [36] Everyone who has faith in the Son has eternal life. But no one who rejects him will ever share in that life, and God will be angry with them forever.

4 Jesus knew that the Pharisees had heard that he was winning and baptizing more followers than John was. [2] But Jesus' disciples were really the ones doing the baptizing, and not Jesus himself.

Jesus and the Samaritan Woman

[3] Jesus left Judea and started for Galilee again. [4] This time he had to go through Samaria, [5] and on his way he came to the town of Sychar. It was near the field that Jacob had long ago given to his son Joseph. [6-8] The well that Jacob had dug was still there, and Jesus sat down beside it because he was tired from traveling. It was noon, and after Jesus' disciples had gone into town to buy some food, a Samaritan woman came to draw water from the well.

Jesus asked her, "Would you please give me a drink of water?"

[9] "You are a Jew," she replied, "and I am a Samaritan woman. How can you ask me for a drink of water when Jews and Samaritans won't have anything to do with each other?"°

[10] Jesus answered, "You don't know what God wants to give you, and you don't know who is asking you for a drink. If you did, you would ask me for the water that gives life."

[11] "Sir," the woman said, "you don't even have a bucket, and the well is deep. Where are you going to get this life-giving water? [12] Our ancestor Jacob dug this well for us, and his family and animals got water from it. Are you greater than Jacob?"

[13] Jesus answered, "Everyone who drinks this water will get thirsty again. [14] But no one who drinks the water I give will ever be thirsty again. The water I give is like a flowing fountain that gives eternal life."

[15] The woman replied, "Sir, please give me a drink of that water! Then I won't get thirsty and have to come to this well again."

[16] Jesus told her, "Go and bring your husband."

[17-18] The woman answered, "I don't have a husband."

"That's right," Jesus replied, "you're telling the truth. You don't have a husband. You have already been married five times, and the man you are now living with isn't your husband."

[19] The woman said, "Sir, I can see that you are a prophet. [20] My ancestors worshiped on this mountain, but you Jews say Jerusalem is the only place to worship."

[21] Jesus said to her:

Believe me, the time is coming when you won't worship the Father either on this mountain or in Jerusalem. [22] You Samaritans don't really know the one you worship. But we Jews do know the God we worship, and by using us, God will save the world. [23] But a time is coming, and it is already here! Even now the true worshipers are being led by the Spirit to worship the Father according to the truth. These are the ones the Father is seeking to worship him. ²⁴ God is Spirit, and those who worship God must be led by the Spirit to worship him according to the truth.

²⁵ The woman said, "I know that the Messiah will come. He is the one we call Christ. When he comes, he will explain everything to us."

²⁶ "I am that one," Jesus told her, "and I am speaking to you now."

²⁷ The disciples returned about this time and were surprised to find Jesus talking with a woman. But none of them asked him what he wanted or why he was talking with her.

²⁸ The woman left her water jar and ran back into town. She said to the people, ²⁹ "Come and see a man who told me everything I have ever done! Could he be the Messiah?" ³⁰ Everyone in town went out to see Jesus.

³¹ While this was happening, Jesus' disciples were saying to him, "Teacher, please eat something."

³² But Jesus told them, "I have food that you don't know anything about."

³³ His disciples started asking each other, "Has someone brought him something to eat?"

³⁴ Jesus said:

My food is to do what God wants! He is the one who sent me, and I must finish the work that he gave me to do. ³⁵ You may say that there are still four months until harvest time. But I tell you to look, and you will see that the fields are ripe and ready to harvest. ³⁶ Even now the harvest workers are receiving their reward by gathering a harvest that brings eternal life. Then everyone who planted the seed and everyone who harvests the crop will celebrate together. ³⁷ So the saying proves true, "Some plant the seed, and others harvest the crop." ³⁸ I am sending you to harvest crops in fields where others have done all the hard work.

³⁹ A lot of Samaritans in that town put their faith in Jesus because the woman had said, "This man told me everything I have ever done." ⁴⁰ They came and asked him to stay in their town, and he stayed on for two days.

⁴¹ Many more Samaritans put their faith in Jesus because of what they heard him say. ⁴² They told the woman, "We no longer have faith in Jesus just because of what you told us. We have heard him ourselves, and we are certain that he is the Savior of the world!"

Jesus Heals an Official's Son

⁴³⁻⁴⁴ Jesus had said, "Prophets are honored everywhere, except in their own country." Then two days later he left ⁴⁵ and went to Galilee. The people there welcomed him, because they had gone to the festival in Jerusalem and had seen everything he had done.

⁴⁶ While Jesus was in Galilee, he returned to the village of Cana, where he had turned the water into wine. There was an official in Capernaum whose son was sick. ⁴⁷ And when the man heard that Jesus had come from Judea, he went and begged him to keep his son from dying.

⁴⁸ Jesus told the official, "You won't have faith unless you see miracles and wonders!"

⁴⁹ The man replied, "Lord, please come before my son dies!"

⁵⁰ Jesus then said, "Your son will live. Go on home to him." The man believed Jesus and started back home.

 Did You Know?

Jesus performed his first miracle in Lebanon. Look it up in John 2:1—12.

⁵¹ Some of the official's servants met him along the road and told him, "Your son is better!" ⁵² He asked them when the boy got better, and they answered, "The fever left him yesterday at one o'clock."

⁵³ The boy's father realized that at one o'clock the day before, Jesus had told him, "Your son will live!" So the man and everyone in his family put their faith in Jesus.

⁵⁴ This was the second miracle that Jesus worked after he left Judea and went to Galilee.

Jesus Heals a Sick Man

5 Later, Jesus went to Jerusalem for another Jewish festival. ² In the city near the sheep gate was a pool with five porches, and its name in Hebrew was Bethzatha.°

³⁻⁴ Many sick, blind, lame, and crippled people were lying close to the pool.°

⁵ Beside the pool was a man who had been sick for 38 years. ⁶ When Jesus saw the man and realized that he had been crippled for a long time, he asked him, "Do you want to be healed?"

⁷ The man answered, "Lord, I don't have anyone to put me in the pool when the water is stirred up. I try to get in, but someone else always gets there first."

⁸ Jesus told him, "Pick up your mat and walk!"

⁹ Right then the man was healed. He picked up his

mat and started walking around. The day on which this happened was a Sabbath.

¹⁰ When the Jewish leaders saw the man carrying his mat, they said to him, "This is the Sabbath! No one is allowed to carry a mat on the Sabbath."

¹¹ But he replied, "The man who healed me told me to pick up my mat and walk."

¹² They asked him, "Who is this man that told you to pick up your mat and walk?" ¹³ But he did not know who Jesus was, and Jesus had left because of the crowd.

¹⁴ Later, Jesus met the man in the temple and told him, "You are now well. But don't sin anymore or something worse might happen to you." ¹⁵ The man left and told the leaders that Jesus was the one who had healed him. ¹⁶ They started making a lot of trouble for Jesus because he did things like this on the Sabbath.

¹⁷ But Jesus said, "My Father has never stopped working, and that is why I keep on working." ¹⁸ Now the leaders wanted to kill Jesus for two reasons. First, he had broken the law of the Sabbath. But even worse, he had said that God was his Father, which made him equal with God.

The Son's Authority

¹⁹ Jesus told the people:

I tell you for certain that the Son cannot do anything on his own. He can do only what he sees the Father doing, and he does exactly what he sees the Father do. ²⁰ The Father loves the Son and has shown him everything he does. The Father will show him even greater things, and you will be amazed. ²¹ Just as the Father raises the dead and gives life, so the Son gives life to anyone he wants to.

²² The Father doesn't judge anyone, but he has made his Son the judge of everyone. ²³ The Father wants all people to honor the Son as much as they honor him. When anyone refuses to honor the Son, that is the same as refusing to honor the Father who sent him. ²⁴ I tell you for certain that everyone who hears my message and has faith in the one who sent me has eternal life and will never be condemned. They have already gone from death to life.

²⁵ I tell you for certain that the time will come, and it is already here, when all of the dead will hear the voice of the Son of God. And those who listen to it will live! ²⁶ The Father has the power to give life, and he has given that same power to the Son. ²⁷ And he has given his Son the right to judge everyone, because he is the Son of Man.

²⁸ Don't be surprised! The time will come when all of the dead will hear the voice of the Son of Man, ²⁹ and they will come out of their graves. Everyone who has done good things will rise to life, but everyone who has done evil things will rise and be condemned.

³⁰ I cannot do anything on my own. The Father sent me, and he is the one who told me how to judge. I judge with fairness, because I obey him, and I don't just try to please myself.

Witnesses to Jesus

³¹ If I speak for myself, there is no way to prove I am telling the truth. ³² But there is someone else who speaks for me, and I know

Donkeys are a traditional and popular mode of transportation along the mountainous Afghanistan and Pakistan border.

what he says is true. [33] You sent messengers to John, and he told them the truth. [34] I don't depend on what people say about me, but I tell you these things so that you may be saved. [35] John was a lamp that gave a lot of light, and you were glad to enjoy his light for a while.

[36] But something more important than John speaks for me. I mean the things that the Father has given me to do! All of these speak for me and prove that the Father sent me.

[37] The Father who sent me also speaks for me, but you have never heard his voice or seen him face to face. [38] You have not believed his message, because you refused to have faith in the one he sent.

[39] You search the Scriptures, because you think you will find eternal life in them. The Scriptures tell about me, [40] but you refuse to come to me for eternal life.

[41] I don't care about human praise, [42] but I do know that none of you love God. [43] I have come with my Father's authority, and you have not welcomed me. But you will welcome people who come on their own. [44] How could you possibly believe? You like to have your friends praise you, and you don't care about praise that the only God can give!

[45] Don't think that I will be the one to accuse you to the Father. You have put your hope in Moses, yet he is the very one who will accuse you. [46] Moses wrote about me, and if you had believed Moses, you would have believed me. [47] But if you don't believe what Moses wrote, how can you believe what I say?

Feeding Five Thousand

6 Jesus crossed Lake Galilee, which was also known as Lake Tiberias. [2] A large crowd had seen him work miracles to heal the sick, and those people went with him. [3-4] It was almost time for the Jewish festival of Passover, and Jesus went up on a mountain with his disciples and sat down.

[5] When Jesus saw the large crowd coming toward him, he asked Philip, "Where will we get enough food to feed all these people?" [6] He said this to test Philip, since he already knew what he was going to do.

[7] Philip answered, "Don't you know that it would take almost a year's wages° just to buy only a little bread for each of these people?"

[8] Andrew, the brother of Simon Peter, was one of the disciples. He spoke up and said, [9] "There is a boy here who has five small loaves of barley bread and two fish. But what good is that with all these people?"

[10] The ground was covered with grass, and Jesus told his disciples to tell everyone to sit down. About 5,000 men were in the crowd. [11] Jesus took the bread in his hands and gave thanks to God.

Then he passed the bread to the people, and he did the same with the fish, until everyone had plenty to eat.

[12] The people ate all they wanted, and Jesus told his disciples to gather up the leftovers, so that nothing would be wasted. [13] The disciples gathered them up and filled twelve large baskets with what was left over from the five barley loaves.

[14] After the people had seen Jesus work this miracle, they began saying, "This must be the Prophet who is to come into the world!" [15] Jesus realized that they would try to force him to be their king. So he went up on a mountain, where he could be alone.

Jesus Walks on the Water

[16] That evening, Jesus' disciples went down to the lake. [17] They got into a boat and started across for Capernaum. Later that evening Jesus had still not come to them, [18] and a strong wind was making the water rough.

[19] When the disciples had rowed for five or six kilometers, they saw Jesus walking on the water. He kept coming closer to the boat, and they were terrified. [20] But he said, "I am Jesus!° Don't be afraid!" [21] The disciples wanted to take him into the boat, but suddenly the boat reached the shore where they were headed.

The Bread That Gives Life

[22] The people who had stayed on the east side of the lake knew that only one boat had been there. They also knew that Jesus had not left in it with his disciples. But the next day [23] some boats from Tiberias sailed near the place where the crowd had eaten the bread for which the Lord had given thanks. [24] They saw that Jesus and his disciples had left. Then they got into the boats and went to Capernaum to look for Jesus. [25] They found him on the west side of the lake and asked, "Rabbi, when did you get here?"

[26] Jesus answered, "I tell you for certain that you are not looking for me because you saw the miracles,° but because you ate all the food you wanted. [27] Don't work for food that spoils. Work for food that gives eternal life. The Son of Man will give you this food, because God the Father has given him the right to do so."

[28] "What exactly does God want us to do?" the people asked.

[29] Jesus answered, "God wants you to have faith in the one he sent."

[30] They replied, "What miracle will you work, so that we can have faith in you? What will you do? [31] For example, when our ancestors were in the desert, they were given manna to eat. It happened just as the Scriptures say, 'God gave them bread from heaven to eat.' "

[32] Jesus then told them, "I tell you for certain that Moses wasn't the one who gave you bread from heaven. My Father is the one who gives you

the true bread from heaven. ³³ And the bread that God gives is the one who came down from heaven to give life to the world."

³⁴ The people said, "Lord, give us this bread and don't ever stop!"

³⁵ Jesus replied:

I am the bread that gives life! No one who comes to me will ever be hungry. No one who has faith in me will ever be thirsty. ³⁶ I have told you already that you have seen me and still do not have faith in me. ³⁷ Everything and everyone that the Father has given me will come to me, and I won't turn any of them away.

³⁸ I didn't come from heaven to do what I want! I came to do what the Father wants me to do. He sent me, ³⁹ and he wants to make certain that none of the ones he has given me will be lost. Instead, he wants me to raise them to life on the last day. ⁴⁰ My Father wants everyone who sees the Son to have faith in him and to have eternal life. Then I will raise them to life on the last day.

⁴¹ The people started grumbling because Jesus had said he was the bread that had come down from heaven. ⁴² They were asking each other, "Isn't he Jesus, the son of Joseph? Don't we know his father and mother? How can he say that he has come down from heaven?"

⁴³ Jesus told them:

Stop grumbling! ⁴⁴ No one can come to me, unless the Father who sent me makes them want to come. But if they do come, I will raise them to life on the last day. ⁴⁵ One of the prophets wrote, "God will teach all of them." And so everyone who listens to the Father and learns from him will come to me.

⁴⁶ The only one who has seen the Father is the one who has come from him. No one else has ever seen the Father. ⁴⁷ I tell you for certain that everyone who has faith in me has eternal life.

⁴⁸ I am the bread that gives life! ⁴⁹ Your ancestors ate manna in the desert, and later they died. ⁵⁰ But the bread from heaven has come down, so that no one who eats it will ever die. ⁵¹ I am that bread from heaven! Everyone who eats it will live forever. My flesh is the life-giving bread that I give to the people of this world.

⁵² They started arguing with each other and asked, "How can he give us his flesh to eat?"

⁵³ Jesus answered:

I tell you for certain that you won't live unless you eat the flesh and drink the blood of the Son of Man. ⁵⁴ But if you do eat my flesh and drink my blood, you will have eternal life, and I will raise you to life on the last day. ⁵⁵ My flesh is the true food, and my blood is the true drink. ⁵⁶ If you eat my flesh and drink my blood, you are one with me, and I am one with you.

⁵⁷ The living Father sent me, and I have life because of him. Now everyone who eats my flesh will live because of me. ⁵⁸ The bread that comes down from heaven isn't like what your ancestors ate. They died, but whoever eats this bread will live forever.

⁵⁹ Jesus was teaching in a synagogue in Capernaum when he said these things.

The Words of Eternal Life

⁶⁰ Many of Jesus' disciples heard him and said, "This is too hard for anyone to understand."

⁶¹ Jesus knew that his disciples were grumbling. So he asked, "Does this bother you? ⁶² What if you should see the Son of Man go up to heaven where he came from? ⁶³ The Spirit is the one who gives life! Human strength can do nothing. The words that I have spoken to you are from that life-giving Spirit. ⁶⁴ But some of you refuse to have faith in me." Jesus said this, because from the beginning he knew who would have faith in him. He also knew which one would betray him.

⁶⁵ Then Jesus said, "You cannot come to me, unless the Father makes you want to come. That is why I have told these things to all of you."

⁶⁶ Because of what Jesus said, many of his disciples turned their backs on him and stopped following him. ⁶⁷ Jesus then asked his twelve disciples if they were going to leave him. ⁶⁸ Simon Peter answered, "Lord, there is no one else that we can go to! Your words give eternal life. ⁶⁹ We have faith in you, and we are sure that you are God's Holy One."

⁷⁰ Jesus told his disciples, "I chose all twelve of you, but one of you is a demon!" ⁷¹ Jesus was talking about Judas, the son of Simon Iscariot.° He would later betray Jesus, even though he was one of the twelve disciples.

Jesus' Brothers Don't Have Faith in Him

7 Jesus decided to leave Judea and to start going through Galilee because the leaders of the people wanted to kill him. ² It was almost time for the Festival of Shelters, ³ and Jesus' brothers said to him, "Why don't you go to Judea? Then your disciples can see what you are doing. ⁴ No one does anything in secret, if they want others to know about them. So let the world know what you are doing!" ⁵ Even Jesus' own brothers had not yet become his followers.

⁶ Jesus answered, "My time hasn't yet come, but your time is always here. ⁷ The people of this world cannot hate you. They hate me, because I tell them that they do evil things. ⁸ Go on to the festival. My time hasn't yet come, and I am not going." ⁹ Jesus said this and stayed on in Galilee.

Jesus at the Festival of Shelters

¹⁰ After Jesus' brothers had gone to the festival, he went secretly, without telling anyone.

¹¹ During the festival the leaders of the people looked for Jesus and asked, "Where is he?" ¹² The crowds even got into an argument about him. Some were saying, "Jesus is a good man," while others were saying, "He is lying to everyone." ¹³ But the people were afraid of their leaders, and none of them talked in public about him.

¹⁴ When the festival was about half over, Jesus went into the temple and started teaching. ¹⁵ The leaders were surprised and said, "How does this man know so much? He has never been taught!"

¹⁶ Jesus replied:

I am not teaching something that I thought up. What I teach comes from the one who sent me. ¹⁷ If you really want to obey God, you will know if what I teach comes from God or from me. ¹⁸ If I wanted to bring honor to myself, I would speak for myself. But I want to honor the one who sent me. That is why I tell the truth and not a lie. ¹⁹ Didn't Moses give you the Law? Yet none of you obey it! So why do you want to kill me?

²⁰ The crowd replied, "You're crazy! What makes you think someone wants to kill you?"

²¹ Jesus answered:

I worked one miracle, and it amazed you. ²² Moses commanded you to circumcise your sons. But it wasn't really Moses who gave you this command. It was your ancestors, and even on the Sabbath you circumcise your sons ²³ in order to obey the Law of Moses. Why are you angry with me for making someone completely well on the Sabbath? ²⁴ Don't judge by appearances. Judge by what is right.

²⁵ Some of the people from Jerusalem were saying, "Isn't this the man they want to kill? ²⁶ Yet here he is, speaking for everyone to hear. And no one is arguing with him. Do you suppose the authorities know that he is the Messiah? ²⁷ But how could that be? No one knows where the Messiah will come from, but we know where this man comes from."

²⁸ As Jesus was teaching in the temple, he shouted, "Do you really think you know me and where I came from? I didn't come on my own! The one who sent me is truthful, and you don't know him. ²⁹ But I know the one who sent me, because I came from him."

³⁰ Some of the people wanted to arrest Jesus right then. But no one even laid a hand on him, because his time had not yet come. ³¹ A lot of people in the crowd put their faith in him and said, "When the Messiah comes, he surely won't perform more miracles than this man has done!"

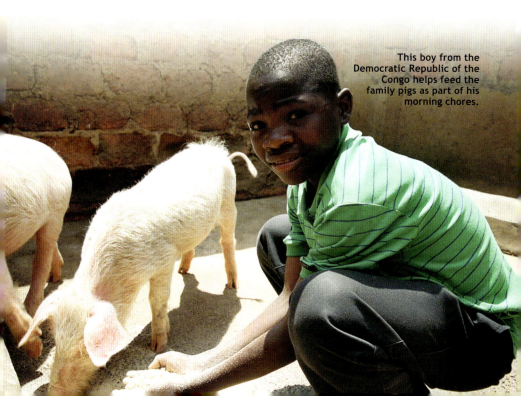

This boy from the Democratic Republic of the Congo helps feed the family pigs as part of his morning chores.

Officers Sent To Arrest Jesus

³² When the Pharisees heard the crowd arguing about Jesus, they got together with the chief priests and sent some temple police to arrest him. ³³ But Jesus told them, "I will be with you a little while longer, and then I will return to the one who sent me. ³⁴ You will look for me, but you won't find me. You cannot go where I am going."

³⁵ The people asked each other, "Where can he go to keep us from finding him? Is he going to some foreign country where our people live? Is he going there to teach the Greeks? ³⁶ What did he mean by saying that we will look for him, but won't find him? Why can't we go where he is going?"

Streams of Life-Giving Water

³⁷ On the last and most important day of the festival, Jesus stood up and shouted, "If you are thirsty, come to me and drink! ³⁸ Have faith in me, and you will have life-giving water flowing from deep inside you, just as the Scriptures say." ³⁹ Jesus was talking about the Holy Spirit, who would be given to everyone that had faith in him. The Spirit had not yet been given to anyone, since Jesus had not yet been given his full glory.

The People Take Sides

⁴⁰ When the crowd heard Jesus say this, some of them said, "He must be the Prophet!" ⁴¹ Others said, "He is the Messiah!" Others even said, "Can the Messiah come from Galilee? ⁴² The Scriptures say that the Messiah will come from the family of King David. Doesn't this mean that he will be born in David's hometown of Bethlehem?" ⁴³ The people started taking sides against each other because of Jesus. ⁴⁴ Some of them wanted to arrest him, but no one laid a hand on him.

The Leaders Refuse To Have Faith in Jesus

⁴⁵ When the temple police returned to the chief priests and Pharisees, they were asked, "Why didn't you bring Jesus here?"

⁴⁶ They answered, "No one has ever spoken like that man!"

⁴⁷ The Pharisees said to them, "Have you also been fooled? ⁴⁸ Not one of the chief priests or the Pharisees has faith in him. ⁴⁹ And these people who don't know the Law are under God's curse anyway."

⁵⁰ Nicodemus was there at the time. He was a member of the council, and was the same one who had earlier come to see Jesus. He said, ⁵¹ "Our Law doesn't let us condemn people before we hear what they have to say. We cannot judge them before we know what they have done."

⁵² Then they said, "Nicodemus, you must be from Galilee! Read the Scriptures, and you will find that no prophet is to come from Galilee."

A Woman Caught in Sin

⁵³ Everyone else went home, but Jesus walked out to the Mount of Olives. **8** ² Then early the next morning he went to the temple. The people came to him, and he sat down and started teaching them.

³ The Pharisees and the teachers of the Law of Moses brought in a woman who had been caught in bed with a man who wasn't her husband. They made her stand in the middle of the crowd. ⁴ Then they said, "Teacher, this woman was caught sleeping with a man who isn't her husband. ⁵ The Law of Moses teaches that a woman like this should be stoned to death! What do you say?"

⁶ They asked Jesus this question, because they wanted to test him and bring some charge against him. But Jesus simply bent over and started writing on the ground with his finger.

⁷ They kept on asking Jesus about the woman. Finally, he stood up and said, "If any of you have never sinned, then go ahead and throw the first stone at her!" ⁸ Once again he bent over and began writing on the ground. ⁹ The people left one by one, beginning with the oldest. Finally, Jesus and the woman were there alone.

¹⁰ Jesus stood up and asked her, "Where is everyone? Isn't there anyone left to accuse you?"

¹¹ "No sir," the woman answered.

Then Jesus told her, "I am not going to accuse you either. You may go now, but don't sin anymore."°

Jesus Is the Light for the World

¹² Once again Jesus spoke to the people. This time he said, "I am the light for the world! Follow me, and you won't be walking in the dark. You will have the light that gives life."

¹³ The Pharisees objected, "You are the only one speaking for yourself, and what you say isn't true!"

¹⁴ Jesus replied:

Even if I do speak for myself, what I say is true! I know where I came from and where I am going. But you don't know where I am from or where I am going. ¹⁵ You judge in the same way that everyone else does, but I don't judge anyone. ¹⁶ If I did judge, I would judge fairly, because I would not be doing it alone. The Father who sent me is here with me. ¹⁷ Your Law requires two witnesses to prove that something is true. ¹⁸ I am one of my witnesses, and the Father who sent me is the other one.

¹⁹ "Where is your Father?" they asked.

"You don't know me or my Father!" Jesus answered. "If you knew me, you would know my Father."

²⁰ Jesus said this while he was still teaching in the place where the temple treasures were stored. But no one arrested him, because his time had not yet come.

You Cannot Go Where I Am Going

²¹ Jesus also told them, "I am going away, and you will look for me. But you cannot go where I am going, and you will die with your sins unforgiven."

²² The people asked, "Does he intend to kill himself? Is that what he means by saying we cannot go where he is going?"

²³ Jesus answered, "You are from below, but I am from above. You belong to this world, but I don't. ²⁴ That is why I said you will die with your sins unforgiven. If you don't have faith in me for who I am, you will die, and your sins will not be forgiven."

²⁵ "Who are you?" they asked Jesus.

Jesus answered, "I am exactly who I told you at the beginning. ²⁶ There is a lot more I could say to condemn you. But the one who sent me is truthful, and I tell the people of this world only what I have heard from him."

²⁷ No one understood that Jesus was talking to them about the Father.

²⁸ Jesus went on to say, "When you have lifted up the Son of Man, you will know who I am. You will also know that I don't do anything on my own. I say only what my Father taught me. ²⁹ The one who sent me is with me. I always do what pleases him, and he will never leave me."

³⁰ After Jesus said this, many of the people put their faith in him.

The Truth Will Set You Free

³¹ Jesus told the people who had faith in him, "If you keep on obeying what I have said, you truly are my disciples. ³² You will know the truth, and the truth will set you free."

³³ They answered, "We are Abraham's children! We have never been anyone's slaves. How can you say we will be set free?"

³⁴ Jesus replied:

I tell you for certain that anyone who sins is a slave of sin! ³⁵ And slaves don't stay in the family forever, though the Son will always remain in the family. ³⁶ If the Son gives you freedom, you are free! ³⁷ I know that you are from Abraham's family. Yet you want to kill me, because my message isn't really in your hearts. ³⁸ I am telling you what my Father has shown me, just as you are doing what your father has taught you.

Your Father Is the Devil

³⁹ The people said to Jesus, "Abraham is our father!"

Jesus replied, "If you were Abraham's children, you would do what Abraham did. ⁴⁰ Instead, you want to kill me for telling you the truth that God gave me. Abraham never did anything like that. ⁴¹ But you are doing exactly what your father does."

"Don't accuse us of having someone else as our father!" they said. "We just have one father, and he is God."

⁴² Jesus answered:

If God were your Father, you would love me, because I came from God and only from him. He sent me. I did not come on my own.

⁴³ Why can't you understand what I am talking about? Can't you stand to hear what I am saying? ⁴⁴ Your father is the devil, and you do exactly what he wants. He has always been a murderer and a liar. There is nothing truthful about him. He speaks on his own, and everything he says is a lie. Not only is he a liar himself, but he is also the father of all lies.

⁴⁵ Everything I have told you is true, and you still refuse to have faith in me. ⁴⁶ Can any of you accuse me of sin? If you cannot, why won't you have faith in me? After all, I am telling you the truth. ⁴⁷ Anyone who belongs to God will listen to his message. But you refuse to listen, because you don't belong to God.

Jesus and Abraham

⁴⁸ The people told Jesus, "We were right to say that you are a Samaritan and that you have a demon in you!"

⁴⁹ Jesus answered, "I don't have a demon in me. I honor my Father, and you refuse to honor me. ⁵⁰ I don't want honor for myself. But there is one who wants me to be honored, and he is also the one who judges. ⁵¹ I tell you for certain that if you obey my words, you will never die."

⁵² Then the people said, "Now we are sure that you have a demon. Abraham is dead, and so are the prophets. How can you say that no one who obeys your words will ever die? ⁵³ Are you greater than our father Abraham? He died, and so did the prophets. Who do you think you are?"

⁵⁴ Jesus replied, "If I honored myself, it would mean nothing. My Father is the one who honors me. You claim that he is your God, ⁵⁵ even though you don't really know him. If I said I didn't know him, I would be a liar, just like all of you. But I know him, and I do what he says. ⁵⁶ Your father Abraham was really glad to see me."

⁵⁷ "You are not even 50 years old!" they said. "How could you have seen Abraham?"

⁵⁸ Jesus answered, "I tell you for certain that even before Abraham was, I was, and I am." ⁵⁹ The people picked up stones to kill Jesus, but he hid and left the temple.

Jesus Heals a Man Born Blind

9 As Jesus walked along, he saw a man who had been blind since birth. ² Jesus' disciples asked, "Teacher, why was this man born blind? Was it because he or his parents sinned?"

³ "No, it wasn't!" Jesus answered. "But because of his blindness, you will see God work a miracle for him. ⁴ As long as it is day, we must do what the one who sent me wants me to do. When night comes, no one can work. ⁵ While I am in the world, I am the light for the world."

⁶ After Jesus said this, he spit on the ground. He made some mud and smeared it on the man's eyes. ⁷ Then he said, "Go and wash off the mud in

Siloam Pool." The man went and washed in Siloam, which means "One Who Is Sent." When he had washed off the mud, he could see.

⁸ The man's neighbors and the people who had seen him begging wondered if he really could be the same man. ⁹ Some of them said he was the same beggar, while others said he only looked like him. But he told them, "I am that man."

¹⁰ "Then how can you see?" they asked.

¹¹ He answered, "Someone named Jesus made some mud and smeared it on my eyes. He told me to go and wash it off in Siloam Pool. When I did, I could see."

¹² "Where is he now?" they asked.

"I don't know," he answered.

The Pharisees Try To Find Out What Happened

¹³⁻¹⁴ The day when Jesus made the mud and healed the man was a Sabbath. So the people took the man to the Pharisees. ¹⁵ They asked him how he was able to see, and he answered, "Jesus made some mud and smeared it on my eyes. Then after I washed it off, I could see."

¹⁶ Some of the Pharisees said, "This man Jesus doesn't come from God. If he did, he would not break the law of the Sabbath."

Others asked, "How could someone who is a sinner work such a miracle?"

Since the Pharisees could not agree among themselves, ¹⁷ they asked the man, "What do you say about this one who healed your eyes?"

"He is a prophet!" the man told them.

¹⁸ But the Jewish leaders would not believe that the man had once been blind. They sent for his parents ¹⁹ and asked them, "Is this the son that you said was born blind? How can he now see?"

²⁰ The man's parents answered, "We are certain that he is our son, and we know that he was born blind. ²¹ But we don't know how he got his sight or who gave it to him. Ask him! He is old enough to speak for himself."

²²⁻²³ The man's parents said this because they were afraid of their leaders. The leaders had already agreed that no one was to have anything to do with anyone who said Jesus was the Messiah.

²⁴ The leaders called the man back and said, "Swear by God to tell the truth! We know that Jesus is a sinner."

²⁵ The man replied, "I don't know if he is a sinner or not. All I know is that I used to be blind, but now I can see!"

²⁶ "What did he do to you?" they asked. "How did he heal your eyes?"

²⁷ The man answered, "I have already told you once, and you refused to listen. Why do you want me to tell you again? Do you also want to become his disciples?"

²⁸ The leaders insulted the man and said, "You are his follower! We are followers of Moses. ²⁹ We are sure that God spoke to Moses, but we don't even know where Jesus comes from."

³⁰ "How strange!" the man replied. "He healed my eyes, and yet you don't know where he comes from. ³¹ We know that God listens only to people who love and obey him. God doesn't listen to sinners. ³² And this is the first time in history that anyone has ever given sight to someone born blind. ³³ Jesus could not do anything unless he came from God."

³⁴ The leaders told the man, "You have been a sinner since the day you were born! Do you think you can teach us anything?" Then they said, "You can never come back into any of our synagogues!"

³⁵ When Jesus heard what had happened, he went and found the man. Then Jesus asked, "Do you have faith in the Son of Man?"

³⁶ He replied, "Sir, if you will tell me who he is, I will put my faith in him."

³⁷ "You have already seen him," Jesus answered, "and right now he is talking with you."

On their way to school, these children from Nepal stop to take a rest from the steep climb up the Himalayan mountainside.

³⁸ The man said, "Lord, I put my faith in you!" Then he worshiped Jesus.
³⁹ Jesus told him, "I came to judge the people of this world. I am here to give sight to the blind and to make blind everyone who can see."
⁴⁰ When the Pharisees heard Jesus say this, they asked, "Are we blind?"
⁴¹ Jesus answered, "If you were blind, you would not be guilty. But now that you claim to see, you will keep on being guilty."

A Story about Sheep

10 Jesus said:
I tell you for certain that only thieves and robbers climb over the fence instead of going in through the gate to the sheep pen. ²⁻³ But the gatekeeper opens the gate for the shepherd, and he goes in through it. The sheep know their shepherd's voice. He calls each of them by name and leads them out.
⁴ When he has led out all of his sheep, he walks in front of them, and they follow, because they know his voice. ⁵ The sheep will not follow strangers. They don't recognize a stranger's voice, and they run away.
⁶ Jesus told the people this story. But they did not understand what he was talking about.

Jesus Is the Good Shepherd
⁷ Jesus said:
I tell you for certain that I am the gate for the sheep. ⁸ Everyone who came before me was a thief or a robber, and the sheep did not listen to any of them. ⁹ I am the gate. All who come in through me will be saved. Through me they will come and go and find pasture.
¹⁰ A thief comes only to rob, kill, and destroy. I came so that everyone would have life, and have it fully. ¹¹ I am the good shepherd, and the good shepherd gives up his life for his sheep. ¹² Hired workers are not like the shepherd. They don't own the sheep, and when they see a wolf coming, they run off and leave the sheep. Then the wolf attacks and scatters the flock. ¹³ Hired workers run away because they don't care about the sheep.
¹⁴ I am the good shepherd. I know my sheep, and they know me. ¹⁵ Just as the Father knows me, I know the Father, and I give up my life for my sheep. ¹⁶ I have other sheep that are not in this sheep pen. I must bring them together too, when they hear my voice. Then there will be one flock of sheep and one shepherd.
¹⁷ The Father loves me, because I give up my life, so that I may receive it back again. ¹⁸ No one takes my life from me. I give it up willingly! I have the power to give it up and the power to receive it back again, just as my Father commanded me to do.

¹⁹ The people took sides because of what Jesus had told them. ²⁰ Many of them said, "He has a demon in him! He is crazy! Why listen to him?"
²¹ But others said, "How could anyone with a demon in him say these things? No one like that could give sight to a blind person!"

Jesus Is Rejected
²² That winter, Jesus was in Jerusalem for the Temple Festival. ²³ One day he was walking in that part of the temple known as Solomon's Porch, ²⁴ and the people gathered all around him. They said, "How long are you going to keep us guessing? If you are the Messiah, tell us plainly!"
²⁵ Jesus answered:
I have told you, and you refused to believe me. The things I do by my Father's authority show who I am. ²⁶ But since you are not my sheep, you don't believe me. ²⁷ My sheep know my voice, and I know them. They follow me, ²⁸ and I give them eternal life, so that they will never be lost. No one can snatch them out of my hand. ²⁹ My Father gave them to me, and he is greater than all others.° No one can snatch them from his hands, ³⁰ and I am one with the Father.
³¹ Once again the people picked up stones in order to kill Jesus. ³² But he said, "I have shown you many good things that my Father sent me to do. Which one are you going to stone me for?"
³³ They answered, "We are not stoning you because of any good thing you did. We are stoning you because you did a terrible thing. You are just a man, and here you are claiming to be God!"
³⁴ Jesus replied:
In your Scriptures doesn't God say, "You are gods"? ³⁵ You can't argue with the Scriptures, and God spoke to those people and called them gods. ³⁶ So why do you accuse me of a terrible sin for saying that I am the Son of God? After all, it is the Father who prepared me for this work. He is also the one who sent me into the world. ³⁷ If I don't do as my Father does, you should not believe me. ³⁸ But if I do what my Father does, you should believe because of that, even if you don't have faith in me. Then you will know for certain that the Father is one with me, and I am one with the Father.
³⁹ Again they wanted to arrest Jesus. But he escaped ⁴⁰ and crossed the Jordan to the place where John had earlier been baptizing. While Jesus was there, ⁴¹ many people came to him. They were saying, "John didn't work any miracles, but everything he said about Jesus is true." ⁴² A lot of those people also put their faith in Jesus.

The Death of Lazarus

11 ¹⁻² A man by the name of Lazarus was sick in the village of Bethany. He had two sisters, Mary and Martha. This was the same Mary who later poured perfume on the Lord's head and wiped his feet with her hair. ³ The sisters sent a message to the Lord and told him that his good friend Lazarus was sick.

⁴ When Jesus heard this, he said, "His sickness won't end in death. It will bring glory to God and his Son."

⁵ Jesus loved Martha and her sister and brother. ⁶ But he stayed where he was for two more days. ⁷ Then he said to his disciples, "Now we will go back to Judea."

⁸ "Teacher," they said, "the people there want to stone you to death! Why do you want to go back?"

⁹ Jesus answered, "Aren't there twelve hours in each day? If you walk during the day, you will have light from the sun, and you won't stumble. ¹⁰ But if you walk during the night, you will stumble, because you don't have any light." ¹¹ Then he told them, "Our friend Lazarus is asleep, and I am going there to wake him up."

¹² They replied, "Lord, if he is asleep, he will get better." ¹³ Jesus really meant that Lazarus was dead, but they thought he was talking only about sleep.

¹⁴ Then Jesus told them plainly, "Lazarus is dead! ¹⁵ I am glad that I wasn't there, because now you will have a chance to put your faith in me. Let's go to him."

¹⁶ Thomas, whose nickname was "Twin," said to the other disciples, "Come on. Let's go, so we can die with him."

Jesus Brings Lazarus to Life

¹⁷ When Jesus got to Bethany, he found that Lazarus had already been in the tomb four days. ¹⁸ Bethany was less than three kilometers, ¹⁹ and many people had come from the city to comfort Martha and Mary because their brother had died.

²⁰ When Martha heard that Jesus had arrived, she went out to meet him, but Mary stayed in the house. ²¹ Martha said to Jesus, "Lord, if you had been here, my brother would not have died. ²² Yet even now I know that God will do anything you ask."

²³ Jesus told her, "Your brother will live again!"

²⁴ Martha answered, "I know that he will be raised to life on the last day, when all the dead are raised."

²⁵ Jesus then said, "I am the one who raises the dead to life! Everyone who has faith in me will live, even if they die. ²⁶ And everyone who lives because of faith in me will never really die. Do you believe this?"

²⁷ "Yes, Lord!" she replied. "I believe that you are Christ, the Son of God. You are the one we hoped would come into the world."

²⁸ After Martha said this, she went and privately said to her sister Mary, "The Teacher is here, and he wants to see you." ²⁹ As soon as Mary heard

this, she got up and went out to Jesus. ³⁰ He was still outside the village where Martha had gone to meet him. ³¹ Many people had come to comfort Mary, and when they saw her quickly leave the house, they thought she was going out to the tomb to cry. So they followed her.

³² Mary went to where Jesus was. Then as soon as she saw him, she knelt at his feet and said, "Lord, if you had been here, my brother would not have died."

³³ When Jesus saw that Mary and the people with her were crying, he was terribly upset ³⁴ and asked, "Where have you put his body?"

They replied, "Lord, come and you will see."

³⁵ Jesus started crying, ³⁶ and the people said, "See how much he loved Lazarus."

³⁷ Some of them said, "He gives sight to the blind. Why couldn't he have kept Lazarus from dying?"

³⁸ Jesus was still terribly upset. So he went to the tomb, which was a cave with a stone rolled against the entrance. ³⁹ Then he told the people to roll the stone away. But Martha said, "Lord, you know that Lazarus has been dead four days, and there will be a bad smell."

⁴⁰ Jesus replied, "Didn't I tell you that if you had faith, you would see the glory of God?"

⁴¹ After the stone had been rolled aside, Jesus looked up toward heaven and prayed, "Father, I thank you for answering my prayer. ⁴² I know that you always answer my prayers. But I said this, so that the people here would believe that you sent me."

⁴³ When Jesus had finished praying, he shouted, "Lazarus, come out!" ⁴⁴ The man who had been dead came out. His hands and feet were wrapped with strips of burial cloth, and a cloth covered his face.

Jesus then told the people, "Untie him and let him go."

The Plot To Kill Jesus

⁴⁵ Many of the people who had come to visit Mary saw the things that Jesus did, and they put their faith in him. ⁴⁶ Others went to the Pharisees and told what Jesus had done. ⁴⁷ Then the chief priests and the Pharisees called the council together and said, "What should we do? This man is working a lot of miracles. ⁴⁸ If we don't stop him now, everyone will put their faith in him. Then the Romans will come and destroy our temple and our nation."

⁴⁹ One of the council members was Caiaphas, who was also high priest that year. He spoke up and said, "You people don't have any sense at all! ⁵⁰ Don't you know it is better for one person to die for the people than for the whole nation to be destroyed?" ⁵¹ Caiaphas did not say this on his own. As high priest that year, he was prophesying that Jesus would die for the nation. ⁵² Yet Jesus would not die just for the Jewish nation. He would die to

bring together all of God's scattered people. [53] From that day on, the council started making plans to put Jesus to death.

[54] Because of this plot against him, Jesus stopped going around in public. He went to the town of Ephraim, which was near the desert, and he stayed there with his disciples.

[55] It was almost time for Passover. Many of the Jewish people who lived out in the country had come to Jerusalem to get themselves ready for the festival. [56] They looked around for Jesus. Then when they were in the temple, they asked each other, "You don't think he will come here for Passover, do you?"

[57] The chief priests and the Pharisees told the people to let them know if any of them saw Jesus. That is how they hoped to arrest him.

Look it up!

Which of the following activities is the national sport of Thailand?
a. Bowling
b. Soccer
c. Kickboxing
d. Archery

At Bethany

12 Six days before Passover Jesus went back to Bethany, where he had raised Lazarus from death. [2] A meal had been prepared for Jesus. Martha was doing the serving, and Lazarus himself was there.

[3] Mary took a very expensive bottle of perfume° and poured it on Jesus' feet. She wiped them with her hair, and the sweet smell of the perfume filled the house.

[4] A disciple named Judas Iscariot was there. He was the one who was going to betray Jesus, and he asked, [5] "Why wasn't this perfume sold for 300 silver coins and the money given to the poor?" [6] Judas did not really care about the poor. He asked this because he carried the moneybag and sometimes would steal from it.

[7] Jesus replied, "Leave her alone! She has kept this perfume for the day of my burial. [8] You will always have the poor with you, but you won't always have me."

A Plot To Kill Lazarus

[9] A lot of people came when they heard that Jesus was there. They also wanted to see Lazarus, because Jesus had raised him from death. [10] So the chief priests made plans to kill Lazarus. [11] He was the reason that many of the people were turning from them and putting their faith in Jesus.

Jesus Enters Jerusalem

[12] The next day a large crowd was in Jerusalem for Passover. When they heard that Jesus was coming for the festival, [13] they took palm branches and went out to greet him. They shouted,

"Hooray!
God bless the one who comes
in the name of the Lord!
God bless the King
of Israel!"

[14] Jesus found a donkey and rode on it, just as the Scriptures say,

[15] "People of Jerusalem,
don't be afraid!
Your King is now coming,
and he is riding
on a donkey."

[16] At first, Jesus' disciples did not understand. But after he had been given his glory, they remembered all this. Everything had happened exactly as the Scriptures said it would.

[17-18] A crowd had come to meet Jesus because they had seen him call Lazarus out of the tomb. They kept talking about him and this miracle. [19] But the Pharisees said to each other, "There is nothing that can be done! Everyone in the world is following Jesus."

Some Greeks Want To Meet Jesus

[20] Some Greeks had gone to Jerusalem to worship during Passover. [21] Philip from Bethsaida in Galilee was there too. So they went to him and said, "Sir, we would like to meet Jesus." [22] Philip told Andrew. Then the two of them went to Jesus and told him.

The Son of Man Must Be Lifted Up

[23] Jesus said:

The time has come for the Son of Man to be given his glory. [24] I tell you for certain that a grain of wheat that falls on the ground will never be more than one grain unless it dies. But if it dies, it will produce lots of wheat. [25] If you love your life, you will lose it. If you give it up in this world, you will be given eternal life. [26] If you serve me, you must go with me. My servants will be with me wherever I am. If you serve me, my Father will honor you.

[27] Now I am deeply troubled, and I don't know what to say. But I must not ask my Father to keep me from this time of suffering. In fact,

Thailand

◉ **Fact File**

Area: 514,000 sq km
Population: 64,865,523
(0-14 years of age: 15,617,061)
Capital: Bangkok
Languages: Thai, English, and 73 other languages
Fun Fact: The people of Thailand are called Thai.

Bangkok

Thailand is a tropical country in Southeast Asia. In the wet season (July to November), monsoons bring heavy rains causing areas to receive more than 254 cm of rain throughout the year.

Thailand's national sport is kickboxing. Another popular sport is called *takraw*. *Takraw* is a game where the players pass a hard rattan ball back and forth over a net using only their heads, body, and legs.

For special and formal occasions, traditional Thai clothing (made of silk which is embroidered and specially dyed) is worn. Popular classical dance tells an epic tale of a prince in search for his princess. These dance performances feature elaborate costumes and masks.

I came into the world to suffer. ²⁸ So Father, bring glory to yourself.

A voice from heaven then said, "I have already brought glory to myself, and I will do it again!" ²⁹ When the crowd heard the voice, some of them thought it was thunder. Others thought an angel had spoken to Jesus.

³⁰ Then Jesus told the crowd, "That voice spoke to help you, not me. ³¹ This world's people are now being judged, and the ruler of this world is already being thrown out! ³² If I am lifted up above the earth, I will make everyone want to come to me." ³³ Jesus was talking about the way he would be put to death.

³⁴ The crowd said to Jesus, "The Scriptures teach that the Messiah will live forever. How can you say that the Son of Man must be lifted up? Who is this Son of Man?"

³⁵ Jesus answered, "The light will be with you for only a little longer. Walk in the light while you can. Then you won't be caught walking blindly in the dark. ³⁶ Have faith in the light while it is with you, and you will be children of the light."

The People Refuse To Have Faith in Jesus

After Jesus had said these things, he left and went into hiding. ³⁷ He had worked a lot of miracles among the people, but they were still not willing to have faith in him. ³⁸ This happened so that what the prophet Isaiah had said would come true,

"Lord, who has believed
our message?
And who has seen
your mighty strength?"

³⁹ The people could not have faith in Jesus, because Isaiah had also said,

⁴⁰ "The Lord has blinded
the eyes of the people,
and he has made
the people stubborn.
He did this so that they
could not see
or understand,
and so that they
would not turn to the Lord
and be healed."

⁴¹ Isaiah said this, because he saw the glory of Jesus and spoke about him.ᵒ ⁴² Even then, many of the leaders put their faith in Jesus, but they did not tell anyone about it. The Pharisees had already given orders for the people not to have anything to do with anyone who had faith in Jesus. ⁴³ And besides, the leaders liked praise from others more than they liked praise from God.

Jesus Came To Save the World

⁴⁴ In a loud voice Jesus said:

Everyone who has faith in me also has faith in the one who sent me. ⁴⁵ And everyone who has seen me has seen the one who sent me. ⁴⁶ I am the light that has come into the world. No one who has faith in me will stay in the dark.

⁴⁷ I am not the one who will judge those who refuse to obey my teachings. I came to save the people of this world, not to be their judge. ⁴⁸ But everyone who rejects me and my teachings will be judged on the last day by what I have said. ⁴⁹ I don't speak on my own. I say only what the Father who sent me has told me to say. ⁵⁰ I know that his commands will bring eternal life. That is why I tell you exactly what the Father has told me.

Jesus Washes the Feet of His Disciples

13 It was before Passover, and Jesus knew that the time had come for him to leave this world and to return to the Father. He had always loved his followers in this world, and he loved them to the very end.

² Even before the evening meal started, the devil had made Judas, the son of Simon Iscariot, decide to betray Jesus.

³ Jesus knew that he had come from God and would go back to God. He also knew that the Father had given him complete power. ⁴ So during the meal Jesus got up, removed his outer garment, and wrapped a towel around his waist. ⁵ He put some water into a large bowl. Then he began washing his disciples' feet and drying them with the towel he was wearing.

⁶ But when he came to Simon Peter, that disciple asked, "Lord, are you going to wash my feet?"

⁷ Jesus answered, "You don't really know what I am doing, but later you will understand."

⁸ "You will never wash my feet!" Peter replied.

"If I don't wash you," Jesus told him, "you don't really belong to me."

⁹ Peter said, "Lord, don't wash just my feet. Wash my hands and my head."

¹⁰ Jesus answered, "People who have bathed and are clean all over need to wash just their feet. And you, my disciples, are clean, except for one of you." ¹¹ Jesus knew who would betray him. That is why he said, "except for one of you."

¹² After Jesus had washed his disciples' feet and had put his outer garment back on, he sat down again. Then he said:

Do you understand what I have done? ¹³ You call me your teacher and Lord, and you should, because that is who I am. ¹⁴ And if your Lord and teacher has washed your feet, you should do the same for each other. ¹⁵ I have set the example, and you should do for each other exactly what I have done for you. ¹⁶ I tell you for certain that servants are not greater than their master, and messengers are not greater than the one who sent them. ¹⁷ You know these things, and God will bless you, if you do them. ¹⁸ I am not talking about all of you. I know the ones I have chosen. But what the Scriptures say must come true. And they say, "The man who ate with me has turned against me!" ¹⁹ I am telling you this before it all happens. Then when it does happen, you will believe who I am. ²⁰ I tell you for certain that anyone who welcomes my messengers also welcomes me, and anyone who welcomes me welcomes the one who sent me.

Jesus Tells What Will Happen to Him

²¹ After Jesus had said these things, he was deeply troubled and told his disciples, "I tell you for certain that one of you will betray me." ²² They were confused about what he meant. And they just stared at each other.

²³ Jesus' favorite disciple was sitting next to him at the meal, ²⁴ and Simon motioned for that disciple to find out which one Jesus meant. ²⁵ So the disciple leaned toward Jesus and asked, "Lord, which one of us are you talking about?"

²⁶ Jesus answered, "I will dip this piece of bread in the sauce and give it to the one I was talking about."

Then Jesus dipped the bread and gave it to Judas, the son of Simon Iscariot. ²⁷ Right then Satan took control of Judas.

Jesus said, "Judas, go quickly and do what you have to do." ²⁸ No one at the meal understood what Jesus meant. ²⁹ But because Judas was in charge of the money, some of them thought that Jesus had told him to buy something they needed for the festival. Others thought that Jesus had told him to give some money to the poor. ³⁰ Judas took the piece of bread and went out.

It was already night.

The New Command

³¹ After Judas had gone, Jesus said:

Now the Son of Man will be given glory, and he will bring glory to God. ³² Then, after God is given glory because of him, God will bring glory to him, and God will do it very soon. ³³ My children, I will be with you for a little while longer. Then you will look for me, but you won't find me. I tell you just as I told the people, "You cannot go where I am going." ³⁴ But I am giving you a new command. You must love each other, just as I have loved you. ³⁵ If you love each other, everyone will know that you are my disciples.

Peter's Promise

³⁶ Simon Peter asked, "Lord, where are you going?"

Jesus answered, "You can't go with me now, but later on you will."

³⁷ Peter asked, "Lord, why can't I go with you now? I would die for you!"

³⁸ "Would you really die for me?" Jesus asked. "I tell you for certain that before a rooster crows, you will say three times that you don't even know me."

Jesus Is the Way to the Father

14 Jesus said to his disciples, "Don't be worried! Have faith in God and have faith in me.^o ² There are many rooms in my Father's house. I wouldn't tell you this, unless it was true. I am going there to prepare a place for each of you. ³ After I have done this, I will come back and take you with me. Then we will be together. ⁴ You know the way to where I am going."

⁵ Thomas said, "Lord, we don't even know where you are going! How can we know the way?"

⁶ "I am the way, the truth, and the life!" Jesus answered. "Without me, no one can go to the Father. ⁷ If you had known me, you would have known the Father. But from now on, you do know him, and you have seen him."

⁸ Philip said, "Lord, show us the Father. That is all we need."

⁹ Jesus replied:

Philip, I have been with you for a long time. Don't you know who I am? If you have seen me, you have seen the Father. How can you ask me to show you the Father? ¹⁰ Don't you believe that I am one with the Father and that the Father is one with me? What I say isn't said on my own. The Father who lives in me does these things.

¹¹ Have faith in me when I say that the Father is one with me and that I am one with the Father. Or else have faith in me simply because of the things I do. ¹² I tell you for certain that if you have faith in me, you will do the same things that I am doing. You will do even greater things, now that I am going back to the Father. ¹³ Ask me, and I will do whatever you ask. This way the Son will bring honor to the Father. ¹⁴ I will do whatever you ask me to do.

The Holy Spirit Is Promised

¹⁵ Jesus said to his disciples:

If you love me, you will do as I command. ¹⁶ Then I will ask the Father to send you the Holy Spirit who will help^o you and always be with you. ¹⁷ The Spirit will show you what is true. The people of this world cannot accept the Spirit, because they don't see or know him. But you know the Spirit, who is with you and will keep on living in you.

¹⁸ I won't leave you like orphans. I will come back to you. ¹⁹ In a little while the people of this world won't be able to see me, but you will see me. And because I live, you will live. ²⁰ Then you will know that I am one with

the Father. You will know that you are one with me, and I am one with you. ²¹ If you love me, you will do what I have said, and my Father will love you. I will also love you and show you what I am like.

²² The other Judas, not Judas Iscariot, then spoke up and asked, "Lord, what do you mean by saying that you will show us what you are like, but you will not show the people of this world?"

²³ Jesus replied:

If anyone loves me, they will obey me. Then my Father will love them, and we will come to them and live in them. ²⁴ But anyone who doesn't love me, won't obey me. What they have heard me say doesn't really come from me, but from the Father who sent me.

²⁵ I have told you these things while I am still with you. ²⁶ But the Holy Spirit will come and help you, because the Father will send the Spirit to take my place. The Spirit will teach you everything and will remind you of what I said while I was with you.

²⁷ I give you peace, the kind of peace that only I can give. It isn't like the peace that this world can give. So don't be worried or afraid.

²⁸ You have already heard me say that I am going and that I will also come back to you. If you really love me, you should be glad that I am going back to the Father, because he is greater than I am.

²⁹ I am telling you this before I leave, so that when it does happen, you will have faith in me. ³⁰ I cannot speak with you much longer, because the ruler of this world is coming. But he has no power over me. ³¹ I obey my Father, so that everyone in the world might know that I love him.

It is time for us to go now.

Jesus Is the True Vine

15 Jesus said to his disciples:

I am the true vine, and my Father is the gardener. ² He cuts away every branch of mine that doesn't produce fruit. But he trims clean every branch that does produce fruit, so that it will produce even more fruit. ³ You are already clean because of what I have said to you.

⁴ Stay joined to me, and I will stay joined to you. Just as a branch cannot produce fruit unless it stays joined to the vine, you cannot produce fruit unless you stay joined to me. ⁵ I am the vine, and you are the branches. If you stay joined to me, and I stay joined to you, then you will produce lots of fruit. But you cannot do anything without me. ⁶ If you don't stay joined to me, you will be thrown away. You will be like dry branches that are gathered up and burned in a fire.

⁷ Stay joined to me and let my teachings become part of you. Then you can pray for whatever you want, and your prayer will be answered. ⁸ When you become fruitful disciples of mine, my Father will be honored. ⁹ I have loved you, just as my Father has loved me. So remain faithful to my love for you. ¹⁰ If you obey me, I will keep loving you, just as my Father keeps loving me, because I have obeyed him.

¹¹ I have told you this to make you as completely happy as I am. ¹² Now I tell you to love each other, as I have loved you. ¹³ The greatest way to show love for friends is to die for them. ¹⁴ And you are my friends, if you obey me. ¹⁵ Servants don't know what their master is doing, and so I don't speak to you as my servants. I speak to you as my friends, and I have told you everything that my Father has told me.

¹⁶ You did not choose me. I chose you and sent you out to produce fruit, the kind of fruit that will last. Then my Father will give you whatever you ask for in my name.ᵒ ¹⁷ So I command you to love each other.

The World's Hatred

¹⁸ If the people of this world hate you, just remember that they hated me first. ¹⁹ If you belonged to the world, its people would love you. But you don't belong to the world. I have chosen you to leave the world behind, and that is why its people hate you. ²⁰ Remember how I told you that servants are not greater than their master. So if people mistreat me, they will mistreat you. If they do what I say, they will do what you say.

²¹ People will do to you exactly what they did to me. They will do it because you belong to me, and they don't know the one who sent me. ²² If I had not come and spoken to them, they would not be guilty of sin. But now they have no excuse for their sin.

²³ Everyone who hates me also hates my Father. ²⁴ I have done things that no one else has ever done. If they had not seen me do these things, they would not be guilty. But they did see me do these things, and they still hate me and my Father too. ²⁵ That is why the Scriptures are true when they say, "People hated me for no reason."

²⁶ I will send you the Spirit who comes from the Father and shows what is true. The Spirit will help you and will tell you about me. ²⁷ Then you will also tell others about me, because you have been with me from the beginning.

16 I am telling you this to keep you from being afraid. ² You will be chased out of the synagogues. And the time will come when people will kill you and think they are doing God a favor. [3] They will do these things because they don't know either the Father or me. [4] I am saying this to you now, so that when the time comes, you will remember what I have said.

The Work of the Holy Spirit

I was with you at the first, and so I didn't tell you these things. [5] But now I am going back to the Father who sent me, and none of you asks me where I am going. [6] You are very sad from hearing all of this. [7] But I tell you that I am going to do what is best for you. That is why I am going away. The Holy Spirit cannot come to help you until I leave. But after I am gone, I will send the Spirit to you.

[8] The Spirit will come and show the people of this world the truth about sin and God's justice and the judgment. [9] The Spirit will show them that they are wrong about sin, because they didn't have faith in me. [10] They are wrong about God's justice, because I am going to the Father, and you won't see me again. [11] And they are wrong about the judgment, because God has already judged the ruler of this world.

[12] I have much more to say to you, but right now it would be more than you could understand. [13] The Spirit shows what is true and will come and guide you into the full truth. The Spirit doesn't speak on his own. He will tell you only what he has heard from me, and he will let you know what is going to happen. [14] The Spirit will bring glory to me by taking my message and telling it

to you. [15] Everything that the Father has is mine. That is why I have said that the Spirit takes my message and tells it to you.

Sorrow Will Turn into Joy

[16] Jesus told his disciples, "For a little while you won't see me, but after a while you will see me." [17] They said to each other, "What does Jesus mean by saying that for a little while we won't see him, but after a while we will see him? What does he mean by saying that he is going to the Father? [18] What is this 'little while' that he is talking about? We don't know what he means."

[19] Jesus knew that they had some questions, so he said:

You are wondering what I meant when I said that for a little while you won't see me, but after a while you will see me. [20] I tell you for certain that you will cry and be sad, but the world will be happy. You will be sad, but later you will be happy.

[21] When a woman is about to give birth, she is in great pain. But after it is all over, she forgets the pain and is happy, because she has brought a child into the world. [22] You are now very sad. But later I will see you, and you will be so happy that no one will be able to change the way you feel. [23] When that time comes, you won't have to ask me about anything. I tell you for certain that the Father will give you whatever you ask for in my name.° [24] You have not asked for anything in this way before, but now you must ask in my name.° Then it will be given to you, so that you will be completely happy.

[25] I have used examples to explain to you what I have been talking about. But the time will come when I will speak to you plainly about the Father and will no longer use examples like these. [26] You will ask the Father in my name,° and I won't have to ask him for you. [27] God the Father loves you because you love me, and you believe that I have come from him. [28] I came from the Father into the world, but I am leaving the world and returning to the Father.

[29] The disciples said, "Now you are speaking plainly to us! You are not using examples. [30] At last we know that you understand everything, and we don't have any more questions. Now we believe that you truly have come from God."

[31] Jesus replied:

Do you really believe me? [32] The time will come and is already here when all of you will be scattered. Each of you will go back home and leave me by myself. But the Father will be with me, and I won't be alone. [33] I have told you this, so that you might have peace in your hearts because of me. While you are in the world, you will have to suffer. But cheer up! I have defeated the world.

A Bedouin girl from Yemen. Bedouins are known for their generosity and nomadic lifestyle.

Jesus Prays

17 After Jesus had finished speaking to his disciples, he looked up toward heaven and prayed:

Father, the time has come for you to bring glory to your Son, in order that he may bring glory to you. [2] And you gave him power over all people, so that he would give eternal life to everyone you give him. [3] Eternal life is to know you, the only true God, and to know Jesus Christ, the one you sent. [4] I have brought glory to you here on earth by doing everything you gave me to do. [5] Now, Father, give me back the glory that I had with you before the world was created.

[6] You have given me some followers from this world, and I have shown them what you are like. They were yours, but you gave them to me, and they have obeyed you. [7] They know that you gave me everything I have. [8] I told my followers what you told me, and they accepted it. They know that I came from you, and they believe that you are the one who sent me. [9] I am praying for them, but not for those who belong to this world. My followers belong to you, and I am praying for them. [10] All that I have is yours, and all that you have is mine, and they will bring glory to me.

[11] Holy Father, I am no longer in the world. I am coming to you, but my followers are still in the world. So keep them safe by the power of the name that you have given me. Then they will be one with each other, just as you and I are one. [12] While I was with them, I kept them safe by the power you have given me. I guarded them, and not one of them was lost, except the one who had to be lost. This happened so that what the Scriptures say would come true.

[13] I am on my way to you. But I say these things while I am still in the world, so that my followers will have the same complete joy that I do. [14] I have told them your message. But the people of this world hate them, because they don't belong to this world, just as I don't.

[15] Father, I don't ask you to take my followers out of the world, but keep them safe from the evil one. [16] They don't belong to this world, and neither do I. [17] Your word is the truth. So let this truth make them completely yours. [18] I am sending them into the world, just as you sent me. [19] I have given myself completely for their sake, so that they may belong completely to the truth.

[20] I am not praying just for these followers. I am also praying for everyone else who will have faith because of what my followers will say about me. [21] I want all of them to be one with each other, just as I am one with you and you are one with me. I also want them to be one with us. Then the people of this world will believe that you sent me.

[22] I have honored my followers in the same way that you honored me, in order that they may be one with each other, just as we are one. [23] I am one with them, and you are one with me, so that they may become completely one. Then this world's people will know that you sent me. They will know that you love my followers as much as you love me.

[24] Father, I want everyone you have given me to be with me, wherever I am. Then they will see the glory that you have given me, because you loved me before the world was created. [25] Good Father, the people of this world don't know you. But I know you, and my followers know that you sent me. [26] I told them what you are like, and I will tell them even more. Then the love that you have for me will become part of them, and I will be one with them.

Jesus Is Betrayed and Arrested

18 When Jesus had finished praying, he and his disciples crossed the Kidron Valley and went into a garden.[o] [2] Jesus often met there with his disciples, and Judas knew where the place was.

[3-5] Judas had promised to betray Jesus. So he went to the garden with some Roman soldiers and temple police, who had been sent by the chief priests and the Pharisees. They carried torches, lanterns, and weapons. Jesus already knew everything that was going to happen, but he asked, "Who are you looking for?"

They answered, "We are looking for Jesus from Nazareth!"

Jesus told them, "I am Jesus!"[o] [6] At once they all backed away and fell to the ground.

[7] Jesus again asked, "Who are you looking for?"

"We are looking for Jesus from Nazareth," they answered.

[8] This time Jesus replied, "I have already told you that I am Jesus. If I am the one you are looking for, let these others go. [9] Then everything will happen, just as I said, 'I did not lose anyone you gave me.' "

[10] Simon Peter had brought along a sword. He now pulled it out and struck at the servant of the high priest. The servant's name was Malchus, and Peter cut off his right ear. [11] Jesus told Peter, "Put your sword away. I must drink from the cup that the Father has given me."

Jesus Is Brought to Annas

[12] The Roman officer and his men, together with the temple police, arrested Jesus and tied him up. [13] They took him first to Annas, who was the father-in-law of Caiaphas, the high priest that year. [14] This was the same Caiaphas who had told the Jewish leaders, "It is better if one person dies for the people."

Peter Says He Doesn't Know Jesus

¹⁵ Simon Peter and another disciple followed Jesus. That disciple knew the high priest, and he followed Jesus into the courtyard of the high priest's house. ¹⁶ Peter stayed outside near the gate. But the other disciple came back out and spoke to the girl at the gate. She let Peter go in, ¹⁷ but asked him, "Aren't you one of that man's followers?"

"No, I am not!" Peter answered.

¹⁸ It was cold, and the servants and temple police had made a charcoal fire. They were warming themselves around it, when Peter went over and stood near the fire to warm himself.

Jesus Is Questioned by the High Priest

¹⁹ The high priest questioned Jesus about his followers and his teaching. ²⁰ But Jesus told him, "I have spoken freely in front of everyone. And I have always taught in our synagogues and in the temple, where all of our people come together. I have not said anything in secret. ²¹ Why are you questioning me? Why don't you ask the people who heard me? They know what I have said."

²² As soon as Jesus said this, one of the temple police hit him and said, "That's no way to talk to the high priest!"

²³ Jesus answered, "If I have done something wrong, say so. But if not, why did you hit me?" ²⁴ Jesus was still tied up, and Annas sent him to Caiaphas the high priest.

Peter Again Denies that He Knows Jesus

²⁵ While Simon Peter was standing there warming himself, someone asked him, "Aren't you one of Jesus' followers?"

Again Peter denied it and said, "No, I am not!"

²⁶ One of the high priest's servants was there. He was a relative of the servant whose ear Peter had cut off, and he asked, "Didn't I see you in the garden with that man?"

²⁷ Once more Peter denied it, and right then a rooster crowed.

Jesus Is Tried by Pilate

²⁸ It was early in the morning when Jesus was taken from Caiaphas to the building where the Roman governor stayed. But the crowd waited outside. Any of them who had gone inside would have become unclean and would not be allowed to eat the Passover meal.

²⁹ Pilate came out and asked, "What charges are you bringing against this man?"

³⁰ They answered, "He is a criminal! That's why we brought him to you."

³¹ Pilate told them, "Take him and judge him by your own laws."

The crowd replied, "We are not allowed to put anyone to death." ³² And so what Jesus said about his death would soon come true.

³³ Pilate then went back inside. He called Jesus over and asked, "Are you the king of the Jews?"

³⁴ Jesus answered, "Are you asking this on your own or did someone tell you about me?"

³⁵ "You know I'm not a Jew!" Pilate said. "Your own people and the chief priests brought you to me. What have you done?"

³⁶ Jesus answered, "My kingdom doesn't belong to this world. If it did, my followers would have fought to keep me from being handed over to our leaders. No, my kingdom doesn't belong to this world."

³⁷ "So you are a king," Pilate replied.

"You are saying that I am a king," Jesus told him. "I was born into this world to tell about the truth. And everyone who belongs to the truth knows my voice."

³⁸ Pilate asked Jesus, "What is truth?"

Jesus Is Sentenced to Death

Pilate went back out and said, "I don't find this man guilty of anything! ³⁹ And since I usually set a prisoner free for you at Passover, would you like for me to set free the king of the Jews?"

⁴⁰ They shouted, "No, not him! We want Barabbas." Now Barabbas was a terrorist.

19 Pilate gave orders for Jesus to be beaten with a whip. ² The soldiers made a crown out of thorn branches and put it on Jesus. Then they put a purple robe on him. ³ They came up to him and said, "Hey, you king of the Jews!" They also hit him with their fists.

⁴ Once again Pilate went out. This time he said, "I will have Jesus brought out to you again. Then you can see for yourselves that I have not found him guilty."

⁵ Jesus came out, wearing the crown of thorns and the purple robe. Pilate said, "Here is the man!"°

⁶ When the chief priests and the temple police saw him, they yelled, "Nail him to a cross! Nail him to a cross!"

Pilate told them, "You take him and nail him to a cross! I don't find him guilty of anything."

⁷ The crowd replied, "He claimed to be the Son of God! Our Law says that he must be put to death."

⁸ When Pilate heard this, he was terrified. ⁹ He went back inside and asked Jesus, "Where are you from?" But Jesus did not answer.

¹⁰ "Why won't you answer my question?" Pilate asked. "Don't you know that I have the power to let you go free or to nail you to a cross?"

¹¹ Jesus replied, "If God had not given you the power, you couldn't do anything at all to me. But the one who handed me over to you did something even worse."

¹² Then Pilate wanted to set Jesus free. But the crowd again yelled, "If you set this man free, you are no friend of the Emperor! Anyone who claims to be a king is an enemy of the Emperor."

¹³ When Pilate heard this, he brought Jesus out. Then he sat down on the judge's bench at the place known as "The Stone Pavement." In Aramaic this pavement is called "Gabbatha." ¹⁴ It was about noon on the day before Passover, and Pilate said to the crowd, "Look at your king!"

¹⁵ "Kill him! Kill him!" they yelled. "Nail him to a cross!"

"So you want me to nail your king to a cross?" Pilate asked.

The chief priests replied, "The Emperor is our king!" ¹⁶ Then Pilate handed Jesus over to be nailed to a cross.

Jesus Is Nailed to a Cross

Jesus was taken away, ¹⁷ and he carried his cross to a place known as "The Skull." In Aramaic this place is called "Golgotha." ¹⁸ There Jesus was nailed to the cross, and on each side of him a man was also nailed to a cross.

¹⁹ Pilate ordered the charge against Jesus to be written on a board and put above the cross. It read, "Jesus of Nazareth, King of the Jews." ²⁰ The words were written in Hebrew, Latin, and Greek.

The place where Jesus was taken wasn't far from the city, and many of the people read the charge against him. ²¹ So the chief priests went to Pilate and said, "Why did you write that he is King of the Jews? You should have written, 'He claimed to be King of the Jews.'"

²² But Pilate told them, "What is written will not be changed!"

²³ After the soldiers had nailed Jesus to the cross, they divided up his clothes into four parts, one for each of them. But his outer garment was made from a single piece of cloth, and it did not have any seams. ²⁴ The soldiers said to each other, "Let's not rip it apart. We will gamble to see who gets it." This happened so that the Scriptures would come true, which say,

> "They divided up my clothes
> and gambled
>   for my garments."

The soldiers then did what they had decided. ²⁵ Jesus' mother stood beside his cross with her sister and Mary the wife of Clopas. Mary Magdalene was standing there too.° ²⁶ When Jesus saw his mother and his favorite disciple with her, he said to his mother, "This man is now your son." ²⁷ Then he said to the disciple, "She is now your mother." From then on, that disciple took her into his own home.

The Death of Jesus

²⁸ Jesus knew that he had now finished his work. And in order to make the Scriptures come true, he said, "I am thirsty!" ²⁹ A jar of cheap wine was there. Someone then soaked a sponge with the wine and held it up to Jesus' mouth on the stem of a hyssop plant. ³⁰ After Jesus drank the wine, he said, "Everything is done!" He bowed his head and died.

A Spear Is Stuck in Jesus' Side

³¹ The next day would be both a Sabbath and the Passover. It was a special day for the Jewish people, and they did not want the bodies to stay on the crosses during that day. So they asked Pilate to break the men's legs and take their bodies down. ³² The soldiers first broke the legs of the other two men who were nailed there. ³³ But when they came to Jesus, they saw that he was already dead, and they did not break his legs.

³⁴ One of the soldiers stuck his spear into Jesus' side, and blood and water came out. ³⁵ We know this is true, because it was told by someone

Baboons, like these seen in Benin, travel in large groups and spend most of their days looking for food (eggs, fruit, and insects) and their nights sleeping in trees or on cliffs.

who saw it happen. Now you can have faith too. [36] All this happened so that the Scriptures would come true, which say, "No bone of his body will be broken" [37] and, "They will see the one in whose side they stuck a spear."

Jesus Is Buried

[38] Joseph from Arimathea was one of Jesus' disciples. He had kept it secret though, because he was afraid of the Jewish leaders. But now he asked Pilate to let him have Jesus' body. Pilate gave him permission, and Joseph took it down from the cross. [39] Nicodemus also came with about 30 kilograms of spices made from myrrh and aloes. This was the same Nicodemus who had visited Jesus one night. [40] The two men wrapped the body in a linen cloth, together with the spices, which was how the Jewish people buried their dead. [41] In the place where Jesus had been nailed to a cross, there was a garden with a tomb that had never been used. [42] The tomb was nearby, and since it was the time to prepare for the Sabbath, they were in a hurry to put Jesus' body there.

Jesus Is Alive

20 On Sunday morning while it was still dark, Mary Magdalene went to the tomb and saw that the stone had been rolled away from the entrance. [2] She ran to Simon Peter and to Jesus' favorite disciple and said, "They have taken the Lord from the tomb! We don't know where they have put him."

[3] Peter and the other disciple started for the tomb. [4] They ran side by side, until the other disciple ran faster than Peter and got there first. [5] He bent over and saw the strips of linen cloth lying inside the tomb, but he did not go in.

[6] When Simon Peter got there, he went into the tomb and saw the strips of cloth. [7] He also saw the piece of cloth that had been used to cover Jesus' face. It was rolled up and in a place by itself. [8] The disciple who got there first then went into the tomb, and when he saw it, he believed. [9] At that time Peter and the other disciple did not know that the Scriptures said Jesus would rise to life. [10] So the two of them went back to the other disciples.

Jesus Appears to Mary Magdalene

[11] Mary Magdalene stood crying outside the tomb. She was still weeping, when she stooped down [12] and saw two angels inside. They were dressed in white and were sitting where Jesus' body had been. One was at the head and the other was at the foot. [13] The angels asked Mary, "Why are you crying?"

She answered, "They have taken away my Lord's body! I don't know where they have put him." [14] As soon as Mary said this, she turned around and saw Jesus standing there. But she did not know who he was. [15] Jesus asked her, "Why are you crying? Who are you looking for?"

She thought he was the gardener and said, "Sir, if you have taken his body away, please tell me, so I can go and get him."

[16] Then Jesus said to her, "Mary!"

She turned and said to him, "Rabboni." The Aramaic word "Rabboni" means "Teacher."

[17] Jesus told her, "Don't hold on to me! I have not yet gone to the Father. But tell my disciples that I am going to the one who is my Father and my God, as well as your Father and your God." [18] Mary Magdalene then went and told the disciples that she had seen the Lord. She also told them what he had said to her.

Jesus Appears to His Disciples

[19] The disciples were afraid of the Jewish leaders, and on the evening of that same Sunday they locked themselves in a room. Suddenly, Jesus appeared in the middle of the group. He greeted them [20] and showed them his hands and his side. When the disciples saw the Lord, they became very happy.

[21] After Jesus had greeted them again, he said, "I am sending you, just as the Father has sent me." [22] Then he breathed on them and said, "Receive the Holy Spirit. [23] If you forgive anyone's sins, they will be forgiven. But if you don't forgive their sins, they will not be forgiven."

Jesus and Thomas

[24] Although Thomas the Twin was one of the twelve disciples, he wasn't with the others when Jesus appeared to them. [25] So they told him, "We have seen the Lord!"

But Thomas said, "First, I must see the nail scars in his hands and touch them with my finger. I must put my hand where the spear went into his side. I won't believe unless I do this!"

[26] A week later the disciples were together again. This time, Thomas was with them. Jesus came in while the doors were still locked and stood in the middle of the group. He greeted his disciples [27] and said to Thomas, "Put your finger here and look at my hands! Put your hand into my side. Stop doubting and have faith!"

[28] Thomas replied, "You are my Lord and my God!"

[29] Jesus said, "Thomas, do you have faith because you have seen me? The people who have faith in me without seeing me are the ones who are really blessed!"

Why John Wrote His Book

[30] Jesus worked many other miracles for his disciples, and not all of them are written in this book. [31] But these are written so that you will put your faith in Jesus as the Messiah and the Son of God. If you have faith in him, you will have true life.

Jesus Appears to Seven Disciples

21 Jesus later appeared to his disciples along the shore of Lake Tiberias. [2] Simon Peter, Thomas the Twin, Nathanael from Cana in Galilee, and the brothers James and John,° were there, together with two other disciples. [3] Simon Peter said, "I'm going fishing!"

The others said, "We will go with you." They went out in their boat. But they didn't catch a thing that night.

[4] Early the next morning Jesus stood on the shore, but the disciples did not realize who he was. [5] Jesus shouted, "Friends, have you caught anything?"

"No!" they answered.

[6] So he told them, "Let your net down on the right side of your boat, and you will catch some fish."

They did, and the net was so full of fish that they could not drag it up into the boat.

[7] Jesus' favorite disciple told Peter, "It's the Lord!" When Simon heard that it was the Lord, he put on the clothes that he had taken off while he was working. Then he jumped into the water. [8] The boat was only about 100 meters from shore. So the other disciples stayed in the boat and dragged in the net full of fish.

[9] When the disciples got out of the boat, they saw some bread and a charcoal fire with fish on it. [10] Jesus told his disciples, "Bring some of the fish you just caught." [11] Simon Peter got back into the boat and dragged the net to shore. In it were 153 large fish, but still the net did not rip.

[12] Jesus said, "Come and eat!" But none of the disciples dared ask who he was. They knew he was the Lord. [13] Jesus took the bread in his hands and gave some of it to his disciples. He did the same with the fish. [14] This was the third time that Jesus appeared to his disciples after he was raised from death.

Jesus and Peter

[15] When Jesus and his disciples had finished eating, he asked, "Simon son of John, do you love me more than the others do?"°

Simon Peter answered, "Yes, Lord, you know I do!"

"Then feed my lambs," Jesus said.

[16] Jesus asked a second time, "Simon son of John, do you love me?"

Peter answered, "Yes, Lord, you know I love you!"

"Then take care of my sheep," Jesus told him.

[17] Jesus asked a third time, "Simon son of John, do you love me?"

Peter was hurt because Jesus had asked him three times if he loved him. So he told Jesus, "Lord, you know everything. You know I love you."

Jesus replied, "Feed my sheep. [18] I tell you for certain that when you were a young man, you dressed yourself and went wherever you wanted to go. But when you are old, you will hold out your hands. Then others will wrap your belt around you and lead you where you don't want to go."

[19] Jesus said this to tell how Peter would die and bring honor to God. Then he said to Peter, "Follow me!"

Jesus and His Favorite Disciple

[20] Peter turned and saw Jesus' favorite disciple following them. He was the same one who had sat next to Jesus at the meal and had asked, "Lord, who is going to betray you?" [21] When Peter saw that disciple, he asked Jesus, "Lord, what about him?"

[22] Jesus answered, "What is it to you, if I want him to live until I return? You must follow me." [23] So the rumor spread among the other disciples that this disciple would not die. But Jesus did not say he would not die. He simply said, "What is it to you, if I want him to live until I return?"

[24] This disciple is the one who told all of this. He wrote it, and we know he is telling the truth.

[25] Jesus did many other things. If they were all written in books, I don't suppose there would be room enough in the whole world for all the books.

Notes

° **1.5** *put it out*: Or "understood it."

° **1.16** *one blessing after another*: Or "one blessing in place of another."

° **2.11,18,23** *miracle*: The Greek text has "sign." In the Gospel of John the word "sign" is used for the miracle itself and as a way of pointing to Jesus as the Son of God.

° **3.3** *from above*: Or "in a new way." The same Greek word is used in verses 7,31.

° **3.25** *a Jewish man*: Some manuscripts have "some Jewish men."

° **4.9** *won't have anything to do with each other*: Or "won't use the same cups."

° **5.2** *Bethzatha*: Some manuscripts have "Bethesda" and others have "Bethsaida."

° **5.3,4** *pool*: Some manuscripts add, "They were waiting for the water to be stirred, because an angel from the Lord would sometimes come down and stir it. The first person to get into the pool after that would be healed."

° **6.7** *almost a year's wages*: The Greek text has "200 silver coins."

° **6.20** *I am Jesus*: The Greek text has "I am."

° **6.26** *miracles*: The Greek text has "signs" here and "sign" in verse 30. In the Gospel of John the word "sign" is used for the miracle itself and as a way of pointing to Jesus as the Son of God.

° **6.71** *Iscariot*: This may mean "a man from Kerioth";

more probably it means "a man who was a liar" or "a man who was a betrayer."

° **8.11** *don't sin anymore:* Verses 1-11 are not in some manuscripts. In other manuscripts these verses are placed after 7.36 or after 21.25 or after Luke 21.38, with some differences in the text.

° **10.29** *he is greater than all others:* Some manuscripts have "they are greater than all others."

° **12.3** *very expensive bottle of perfume:* The Greek text has "expensive perfume made of pure spikenard."

° **12.41** *he saw the glory of Jesus and spoke about him:* Or "he saw the glory of God and spoke about Jesus."

° **14.1** *Have faith in God and have faith in me:* Or "You have faith in God, so have faith in me."

° **14.16** *help:* The Greek word may mean "comfort," "encourage," or "defend."

° **15.16** *in my name:* Or "because you are my followers."

° **16.23,24** *in my name ... in my name:* Or "as my disciples ... as my disciples."

° **16.26** *in my name:* Or "because you are my followers."

° **18.1** *garden:* The Greek word is usually translated "garden," but probably referred to an olive orchard.

° **18.3-5** *I am Jesus:* The Greek text has "I am."

° **19.5** *"Here is the man!":* Or "Look at the man!"

° **19.25** *Jesus' mother stood beside his cross with her sister and Mary the wife of Clopas. Mary Magdalene was standing there too:* The Greek text may also be understood to include only three women ("Jesus' mother stood beside the cross with her sister, Mary the mother of Clopas. Mary Magdalene was standing there too.") or merely two women ("Jesus' mother was standing there with her sister Mary of Clopas, that is, Mary Magdalene."). "Of Clopas" may mean "daughter of" or "mother of."

° **21.2** *the brothers James and John:* Greek "the two sons of Zebedee."

° **21.15** *more than the others do:* Or "more than you love these things?"